William & Kate

JUST MARRIED!

A Royal Fairytale

About a Prince finding his Princess

Illustrated by Tamara Henderson • Written by Anne Price

Once upon a time
in a land across the sea,
there lived a boy and girl
as different as can be...

Kate

William

Kate is a girl
   just like any other.
She lives in England with
   her father, siblings and mother.

William is a boy
 not like you and me.
His family lives in a castle,
 and his Grandmum is the Queen!

Kate spends her days
playing games and having fun.
William spends his with
his brother Harry and his mum.

Each night at bedtime
while kneeling to pray,
Kate hopes for a prince
"to marry one day."

While William lies in bed
awaiting sweet dreams,
he wishes on a shining star:
"Please bring me a queen."

Tennis

Swimming

Photography

As Kate grows up
there are many things she likes to do—
tennis, swimming and photography,
just to name a few.

Fishing

Swimming

Polo

As William grows up
he is sporty, much like Kate,
and thinks fishing, swimming and polo
are all really great.

While at University in Scotland
something quite magical happened.
Kate met the prince she wished for at eight
and William discovered a queen in Kate.

The two became great mates,
　　and soon enjoyed their first date—
a date that led to many more.
　　Yes, they've found the ones they adore!

They both finish school
   and move on with their lives.
A few years later
   William asks Kate to be his wife.

JUST MARRIED!

April 29th is where our story ends,
and the story of the Prince and Princess begins.
Their wedding was one of tears and laughter,
and we're certain they'll live happily ever after.

The End

Royal Family Finger Puppets

Queen

Prince

Princess